Birds

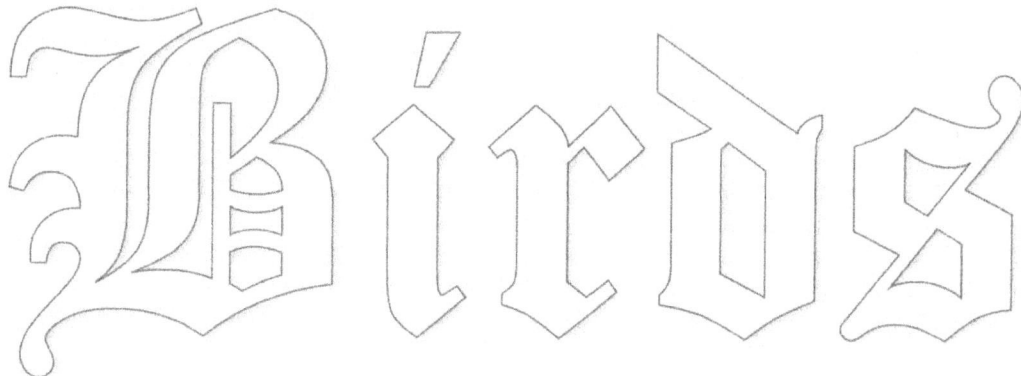

"The air is crowded with birds – beautiful, tender, intelligent birds – to whom life is a song."

George Henry Lewes

Welcome to your very own coloring book created with love. Each picture has been hand drawn with time and consideration so you will be able to gain a sense of relaxation, rest and a wonderful sense of art therapy. Remember to breathe while you are working and creating "your" master piece.

Each drawing has been developed on only one side of the paper so you are able to remove it matt and frame it if you wish. The drawings were also created with very thin lines so that once you add the color many of the lines will disappear.

Thank you for taking this journey with me and giving the gift of peace to yourself.

~Ranada ~ Artist~

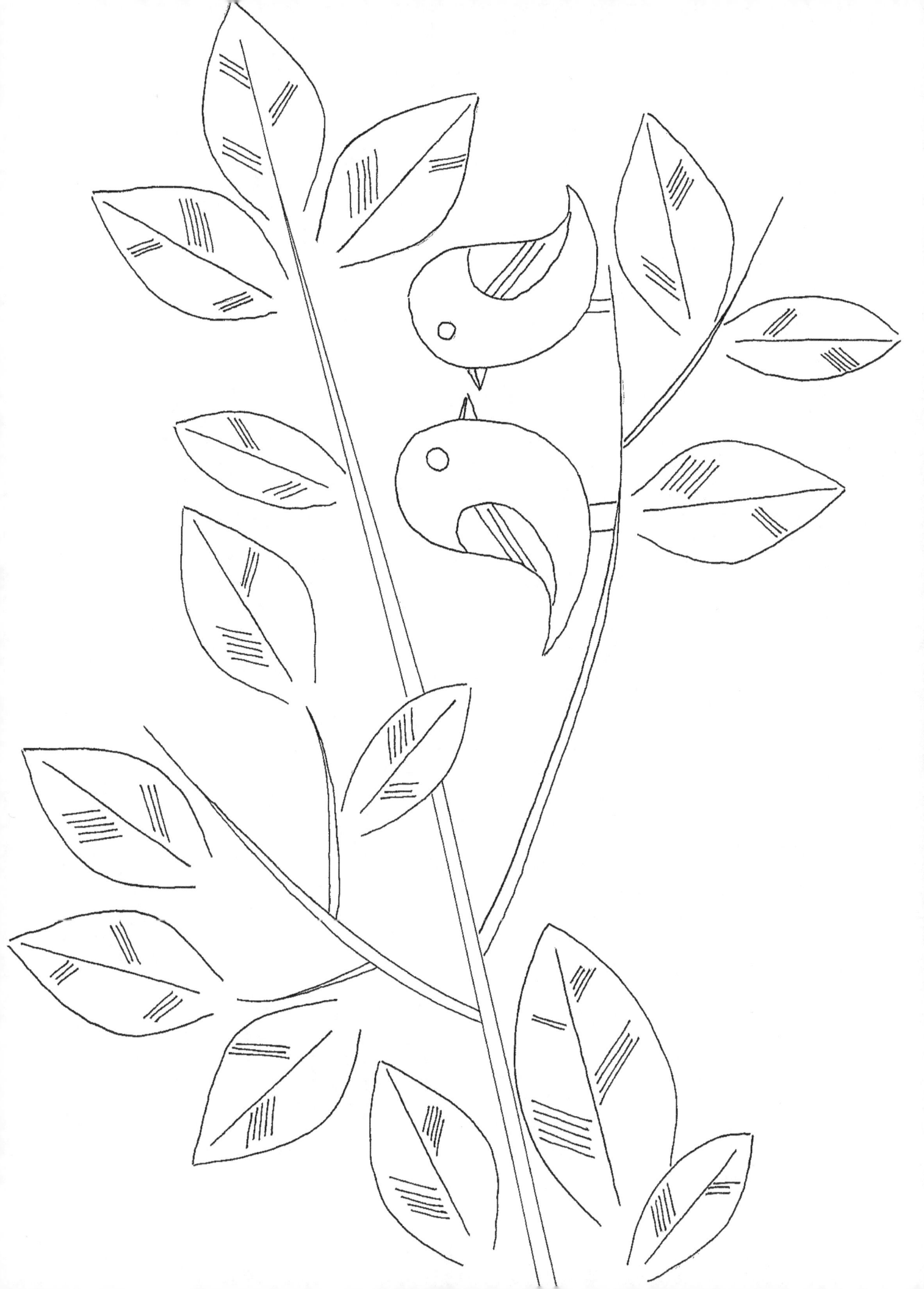

Write things that used to scare you but don't any more.

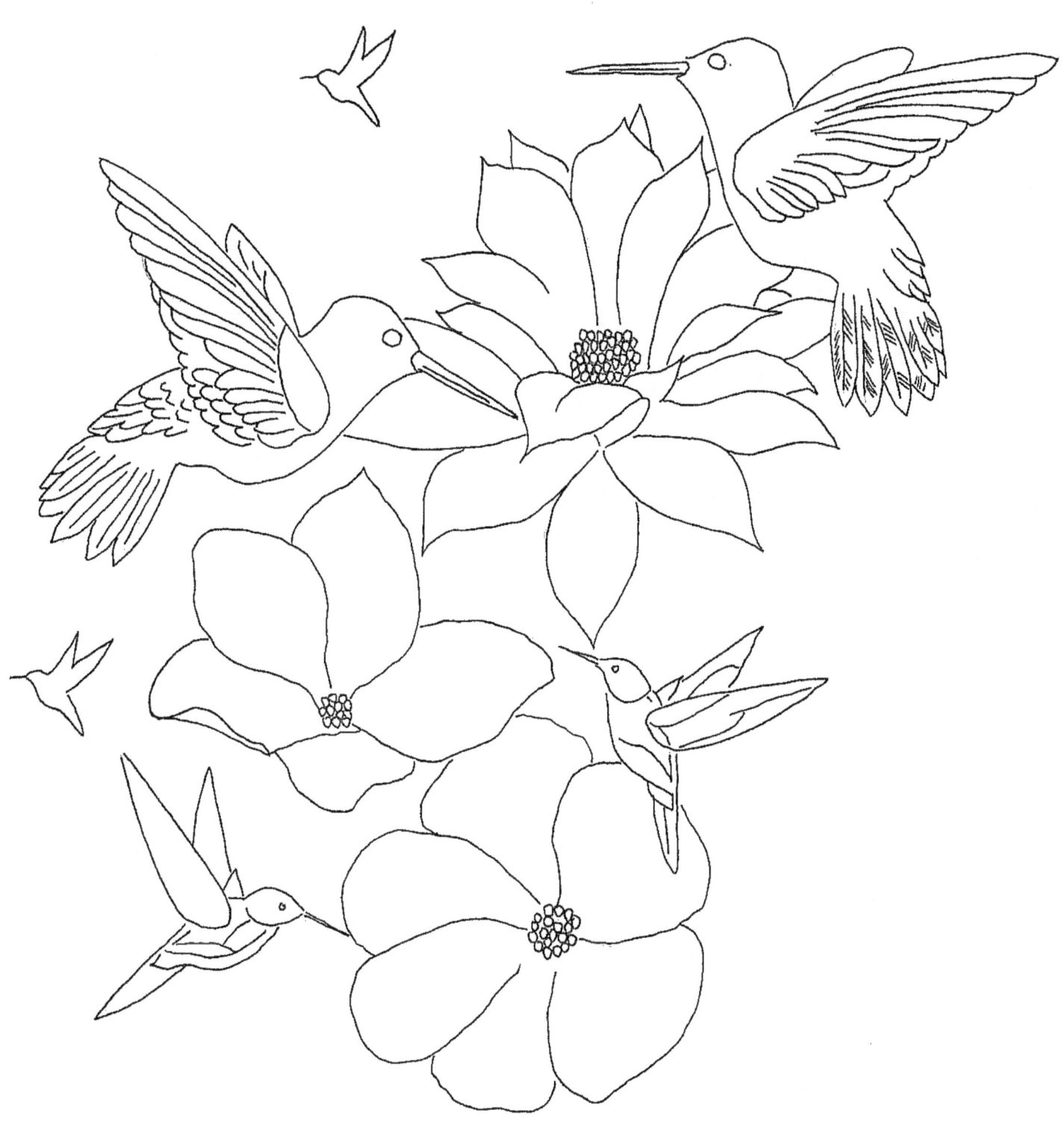

List ways you help others in your journal.

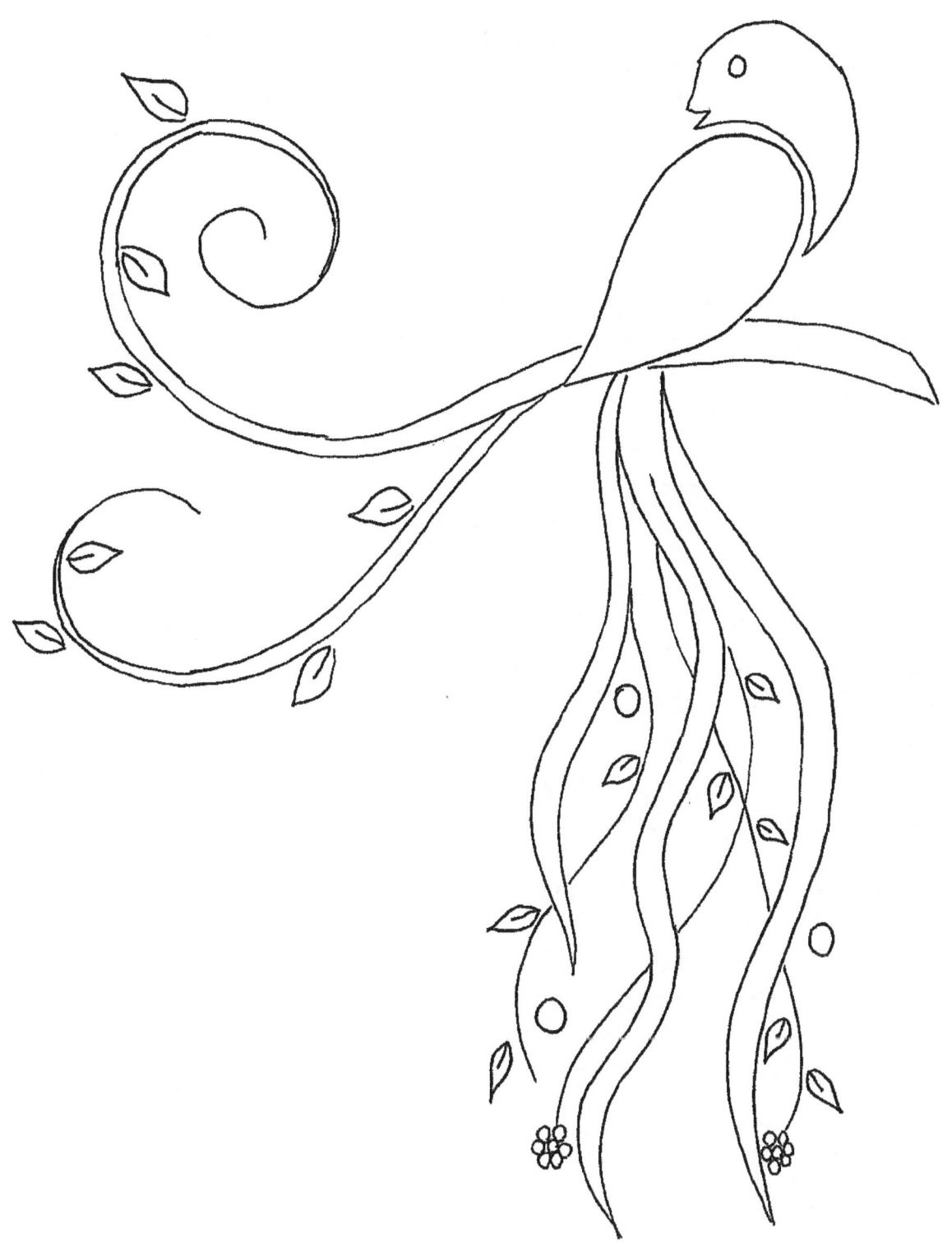

Journaling can be things you like about yourself.

_____
_____
_____
_____
_____
_____
_____
_____
_____
_____
_____
_____
_____
_____
_____
_____
_____
_____
_____
_____
_____
_____
_____

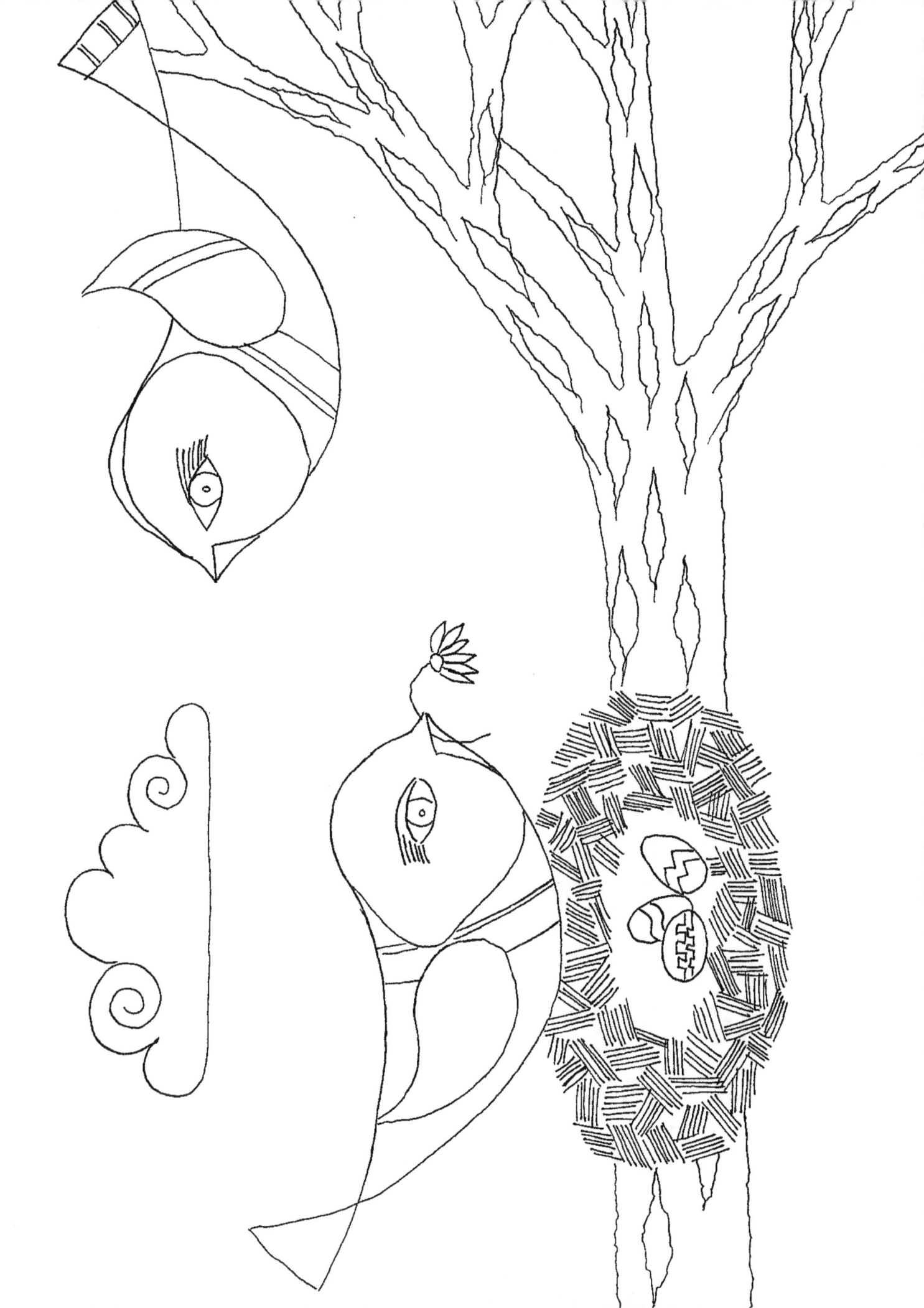

Your journal can be your "bucket list" things to do before you die.

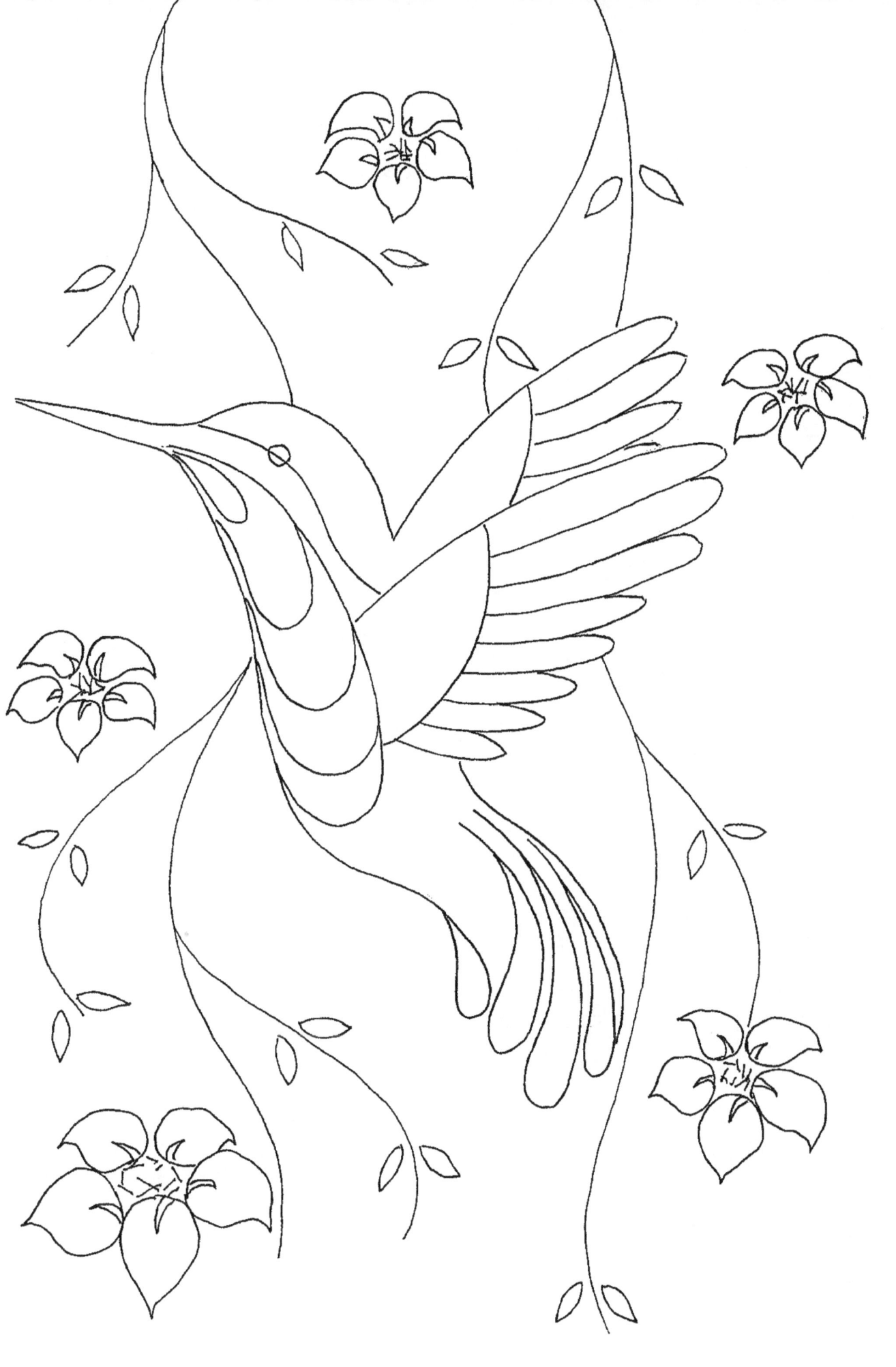

Write ways you can make a difference in your journal.

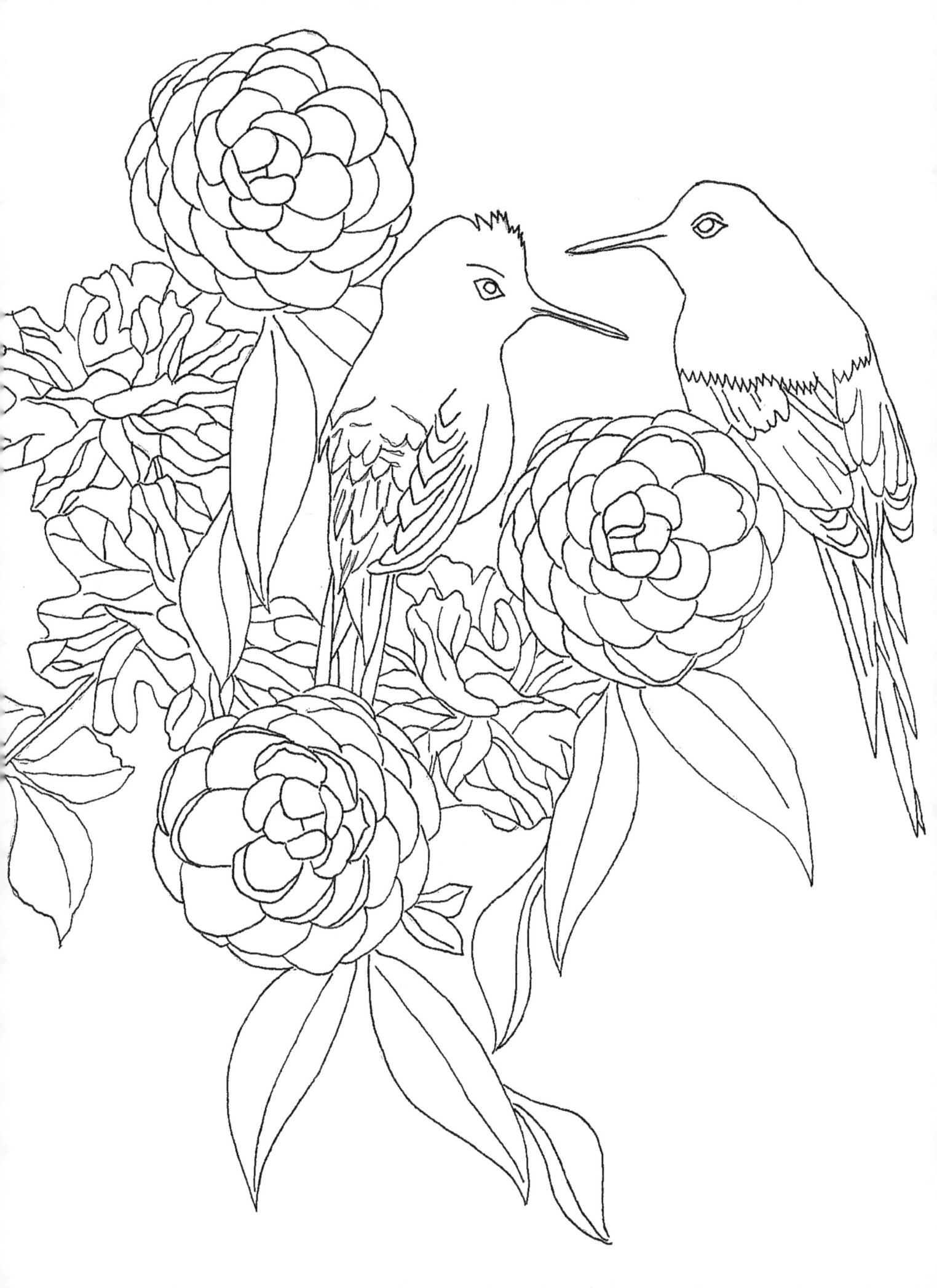

Write about things you believe in, in your journal.

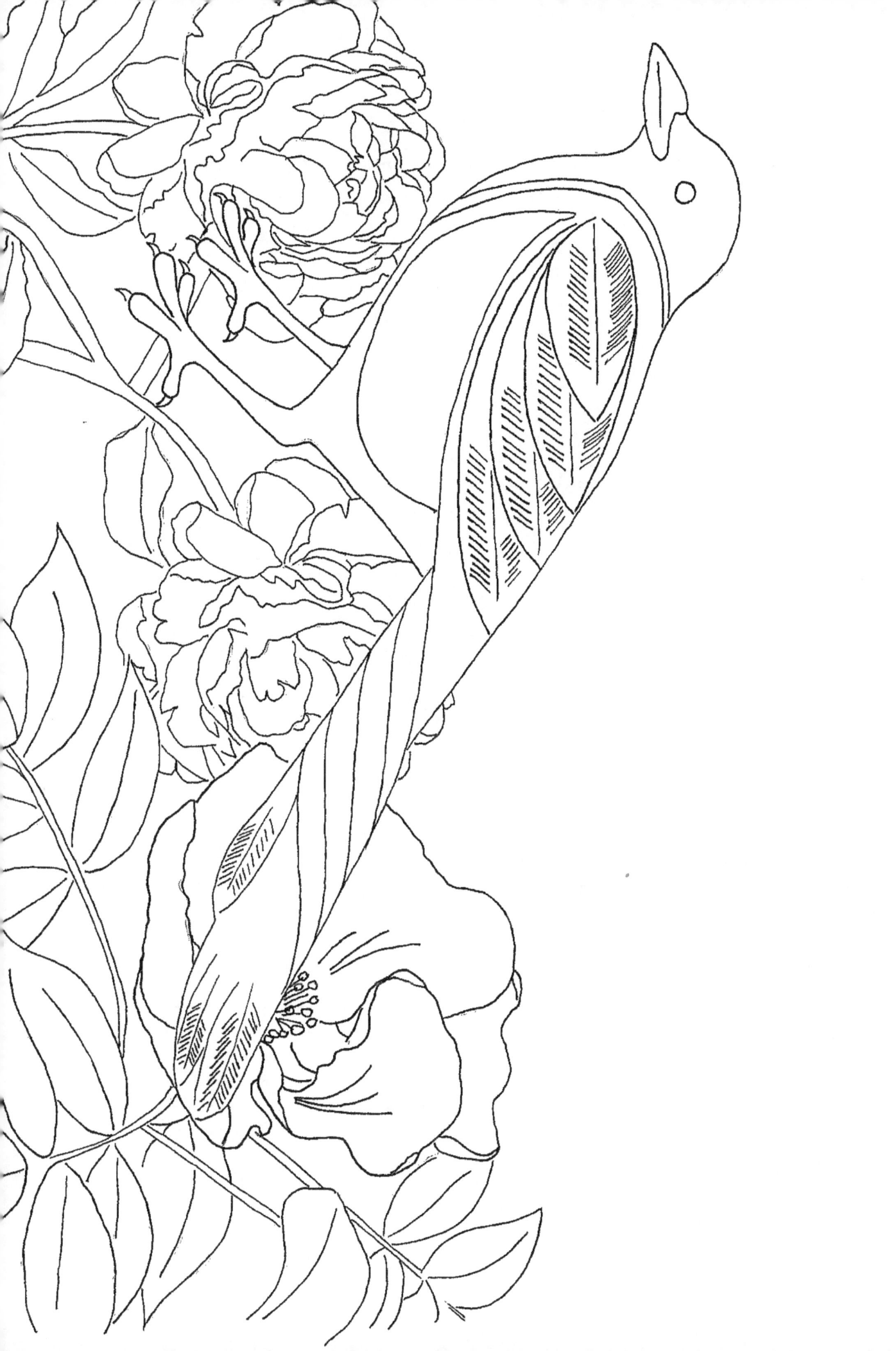

In your journal list some of the jobs you would like to have.

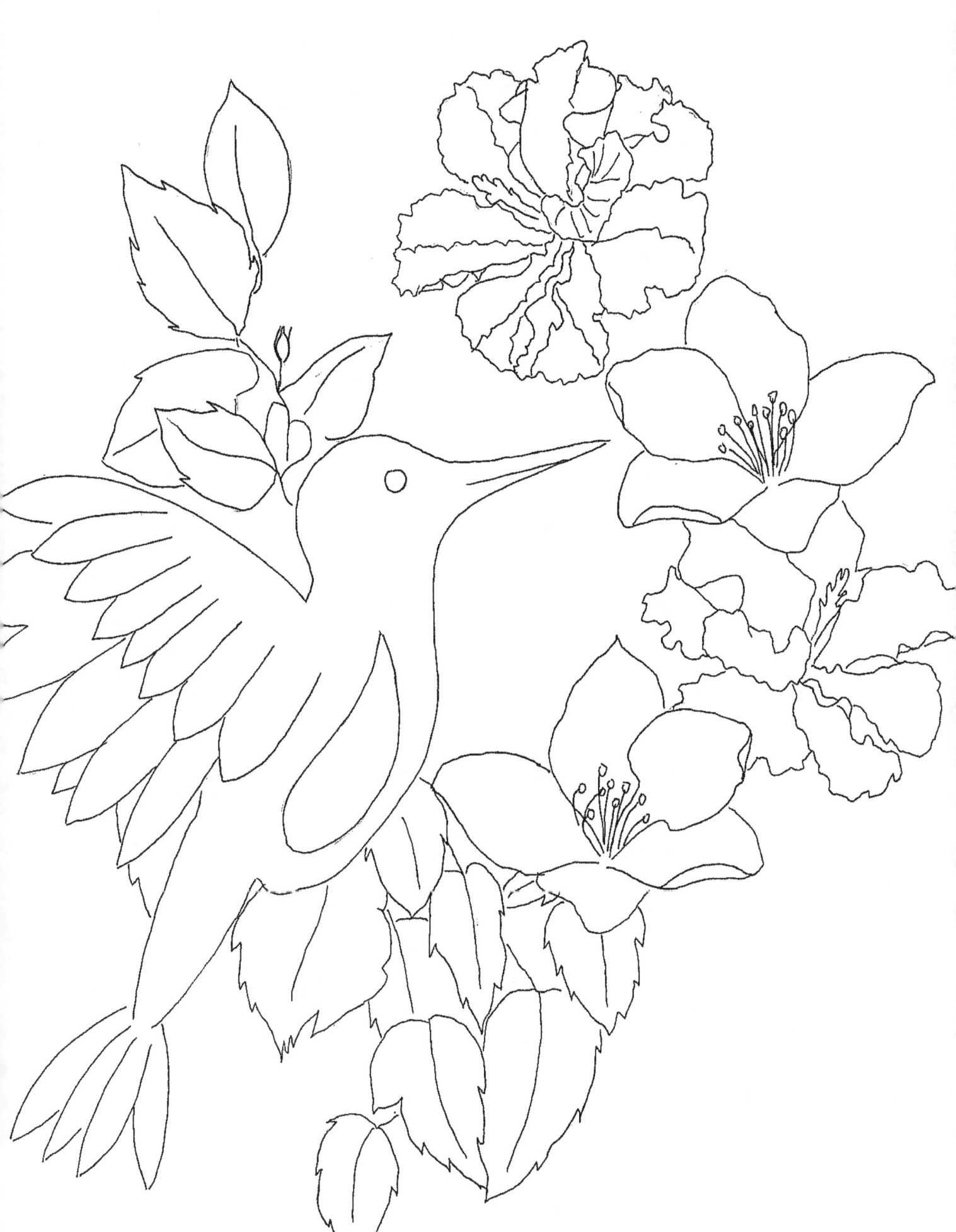

...things that make you laugh.

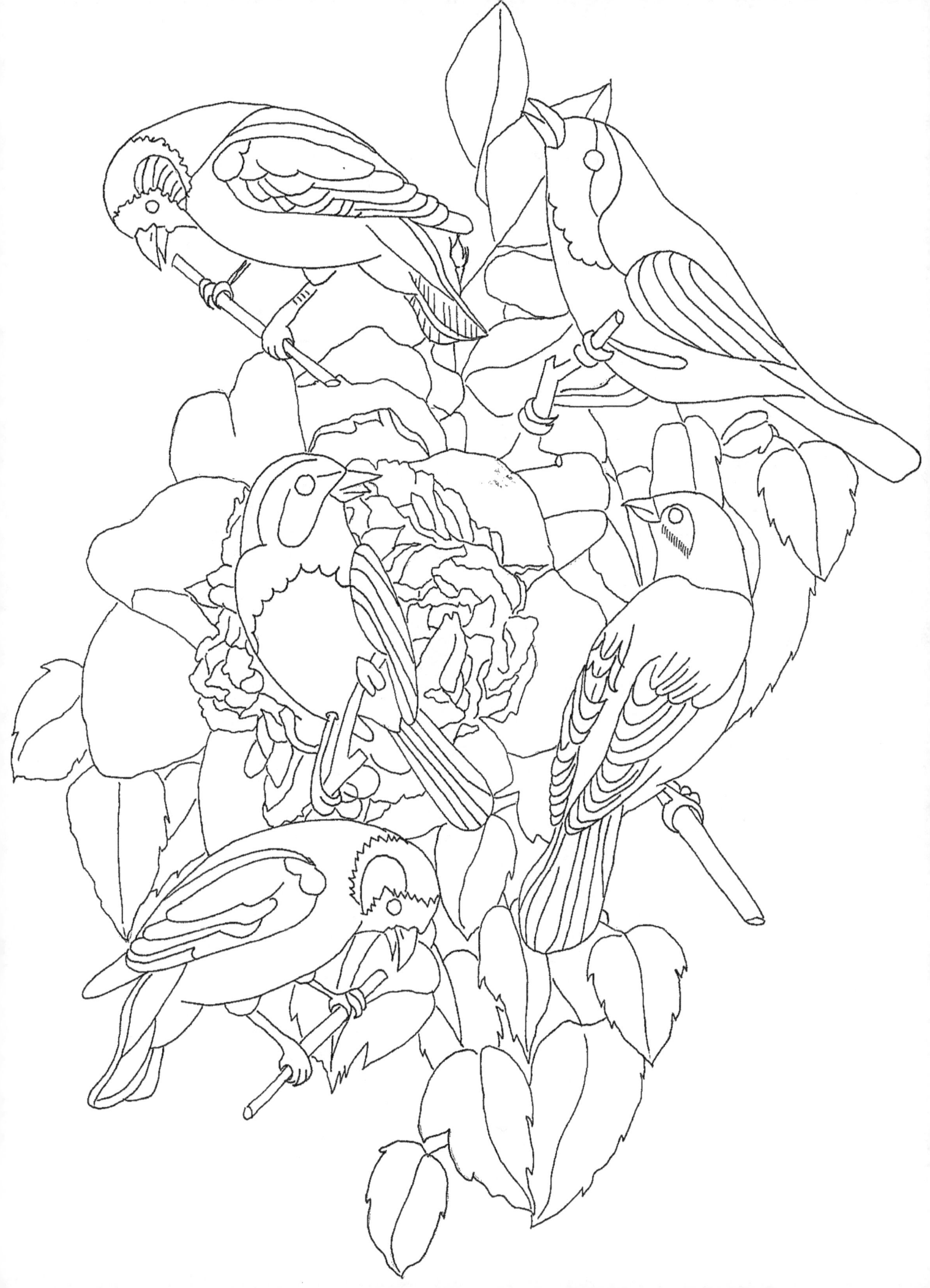

Make a list of things that you find hard to share.

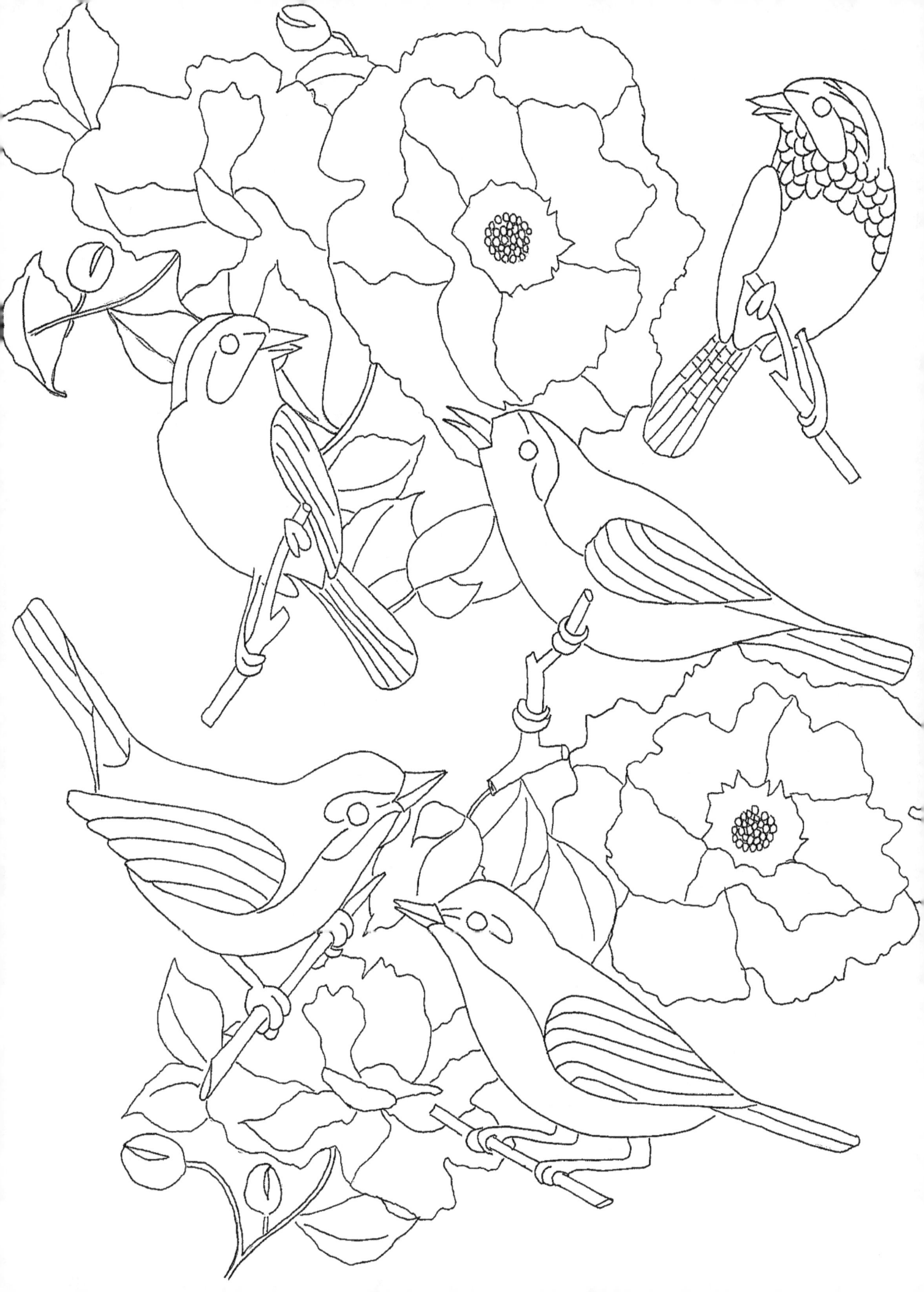

Write down skills and qualities you see in yourself.

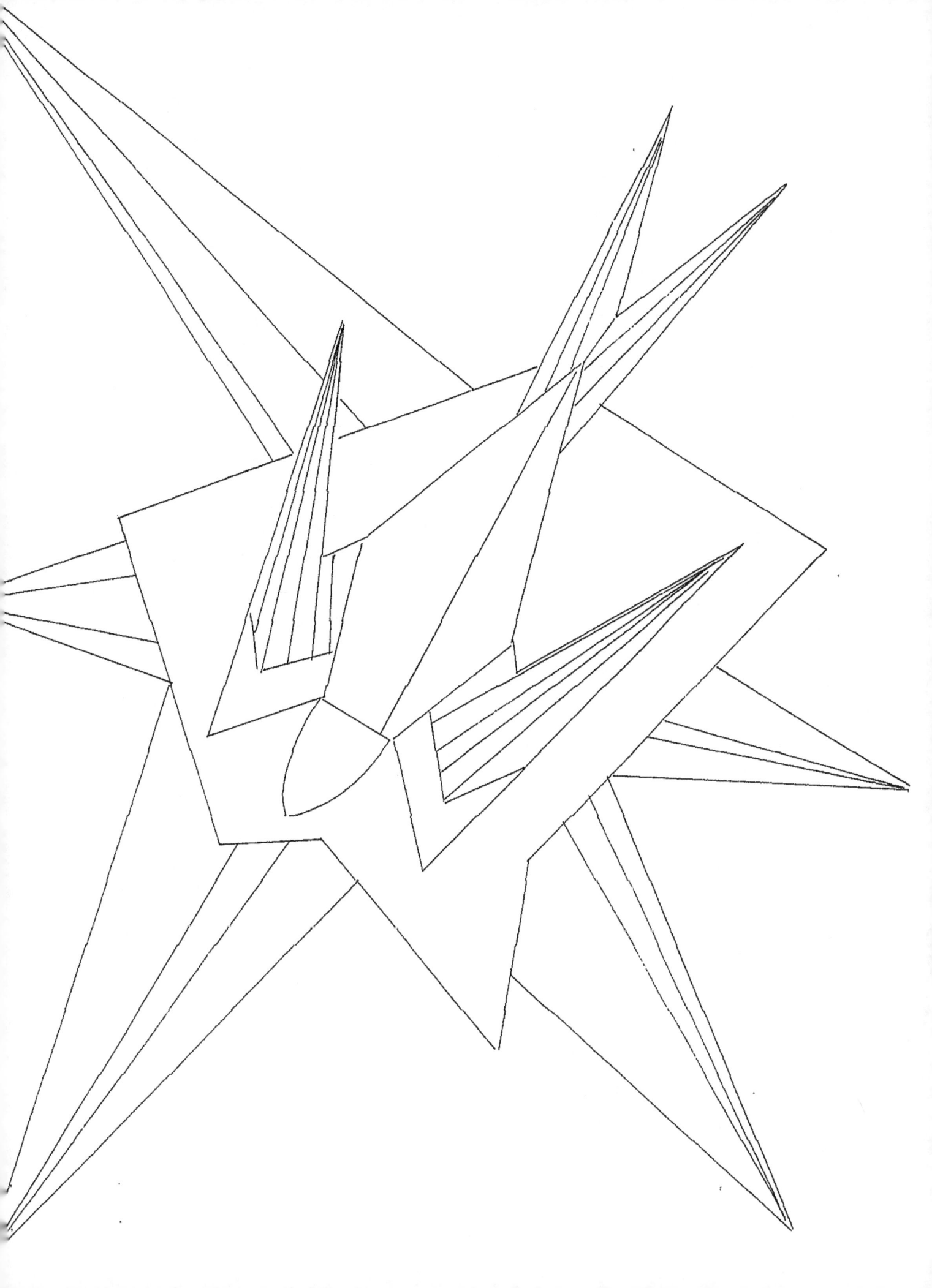

Journal things you would like to do if you had 6 months to live.

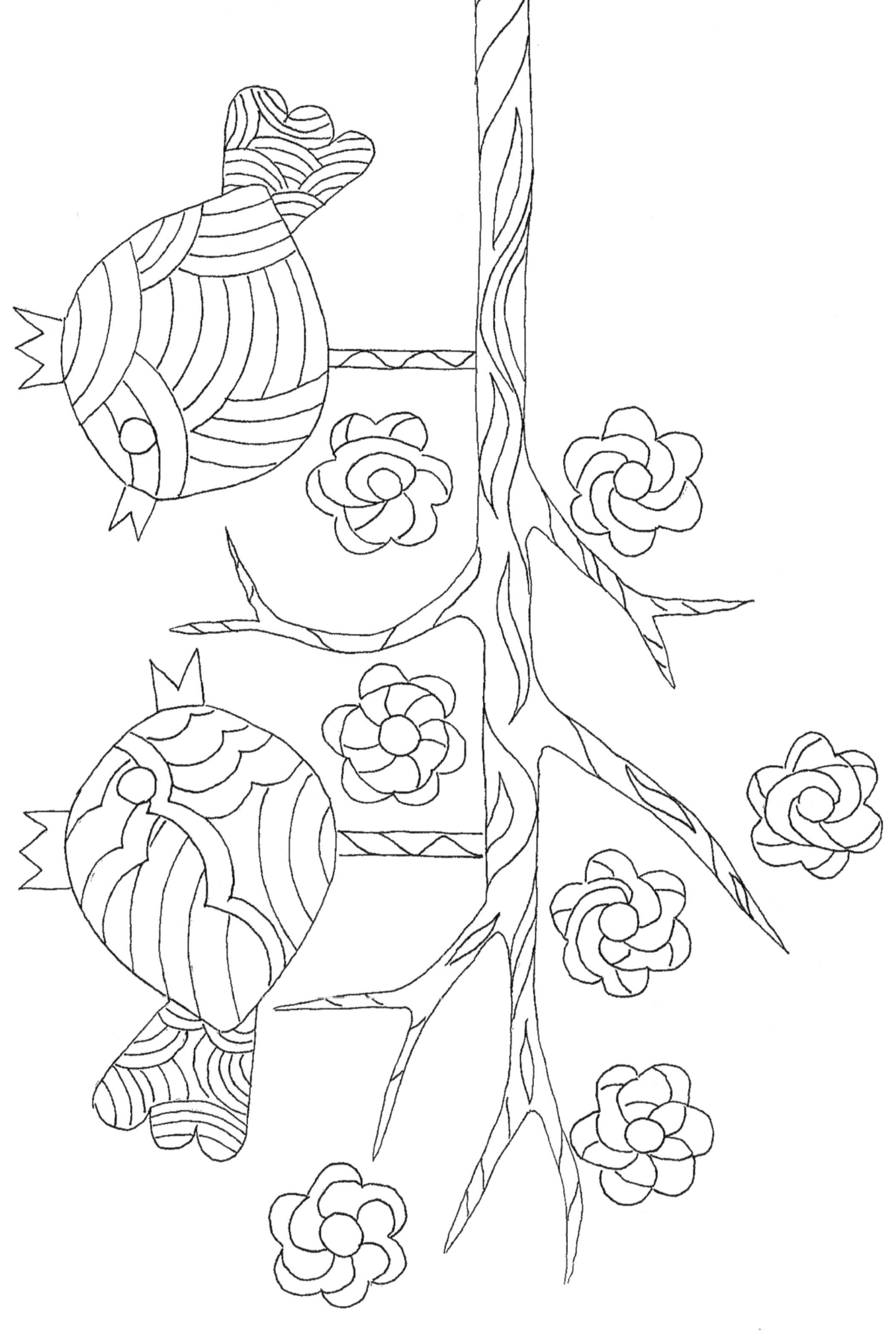

Make a journal list of childhood memories.

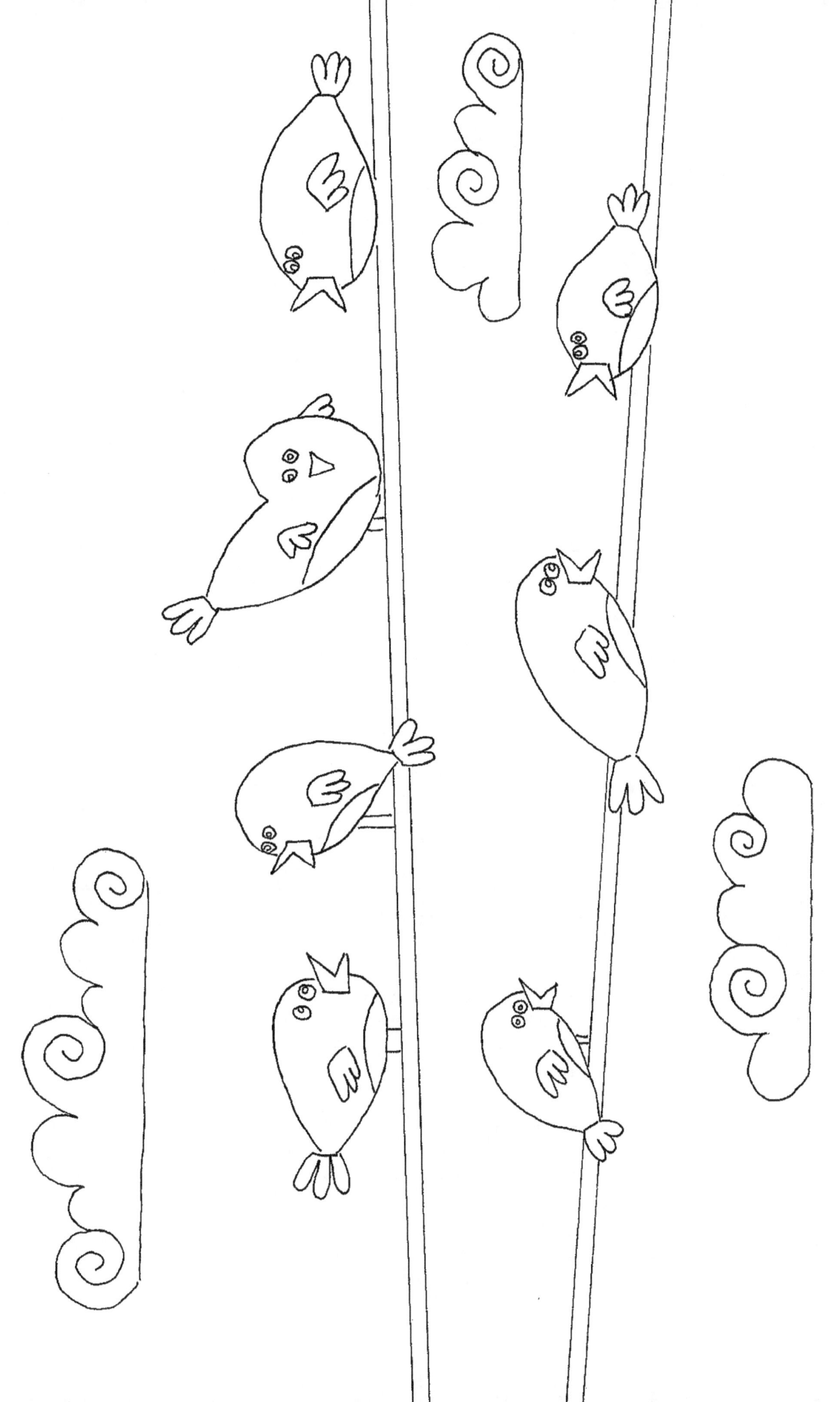

List things you are glad you have done in your lifetime.

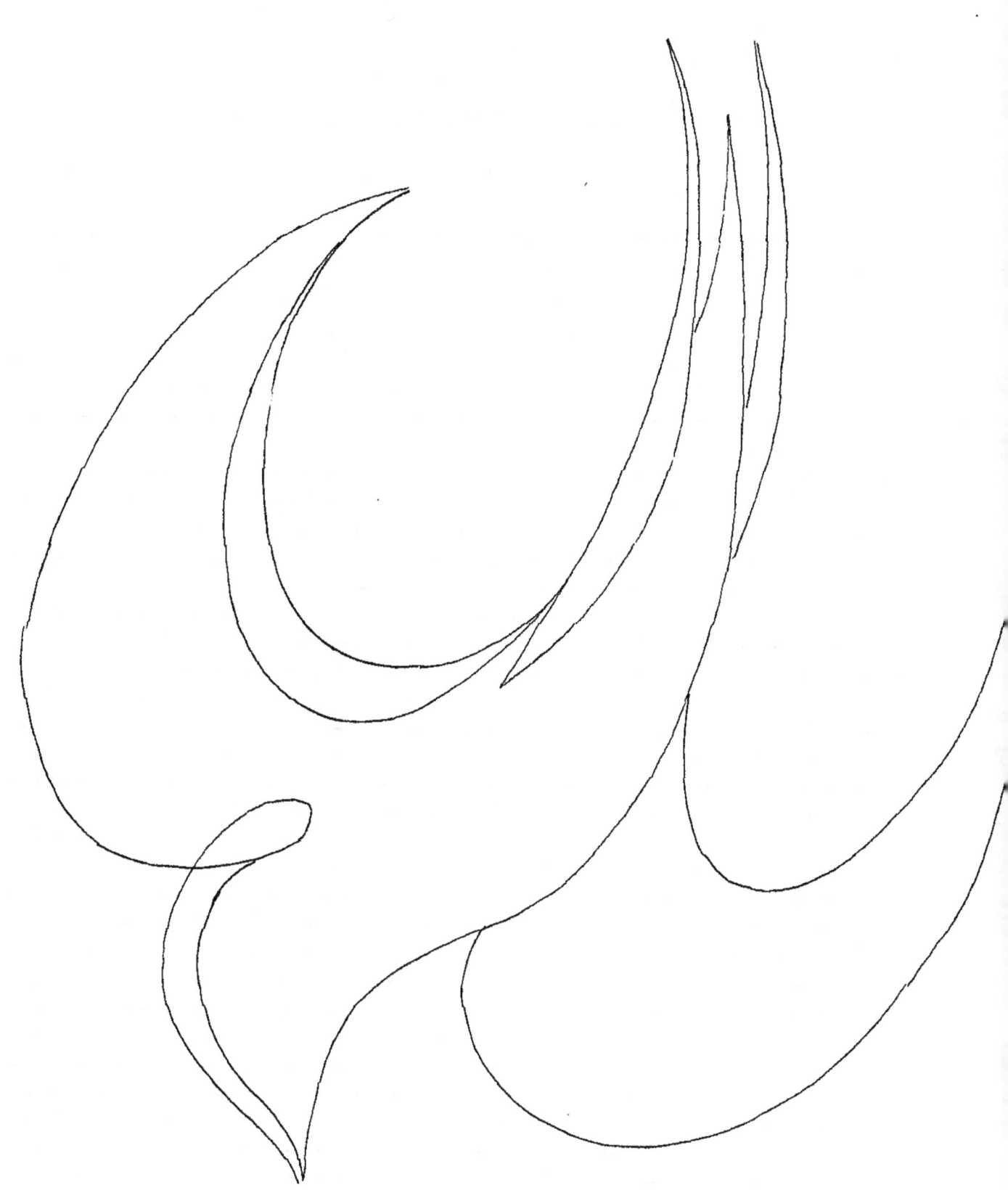

...things that make you cry.

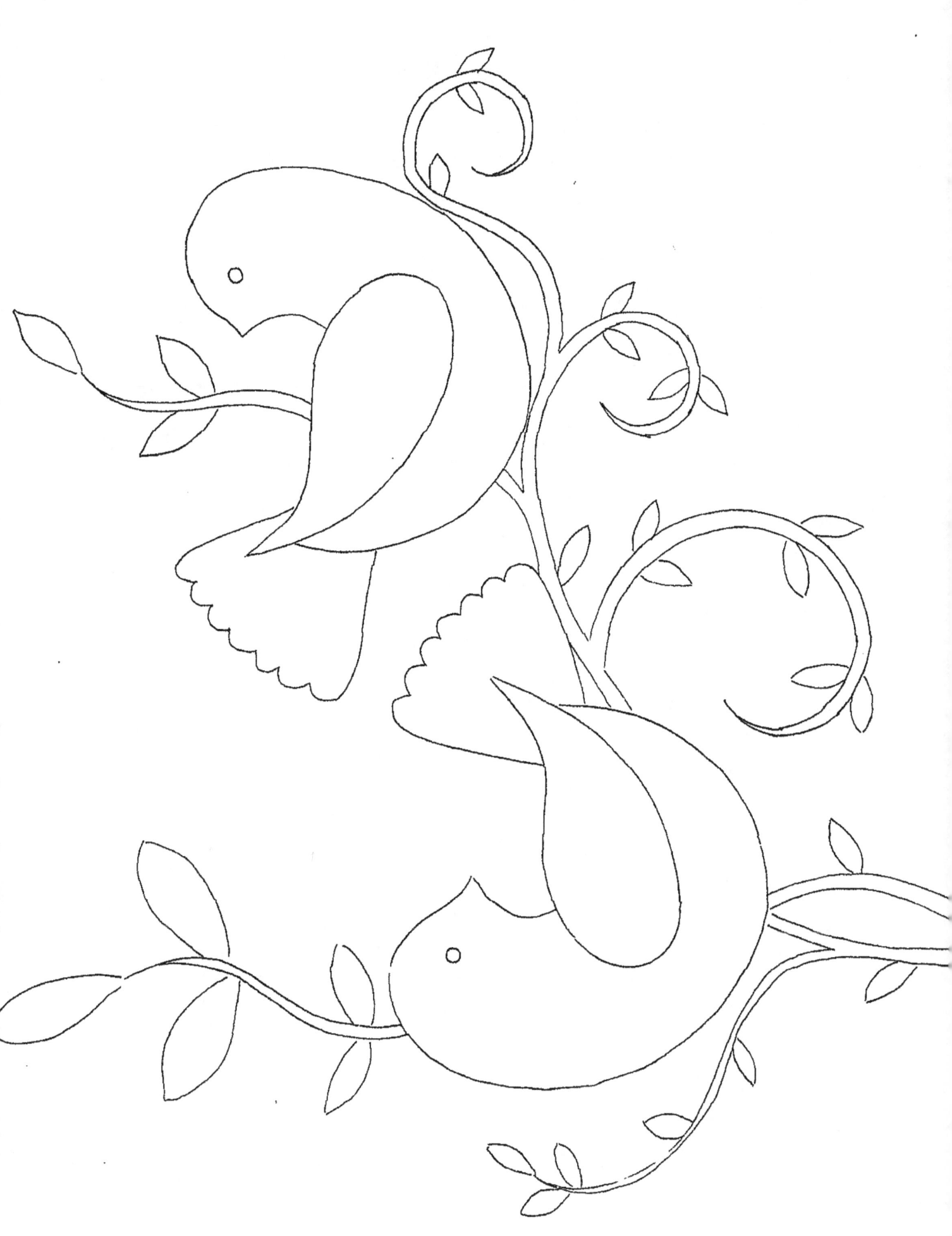

In your journal write things you would like to hear from others.

_____
_____
_____
_____
_____
_____
_____
_____
_____
_____
_____
_____
_____
_____
_____
_____
_____
_____
_____
_____
_____
_____
_____
_____
_____
_____
_____

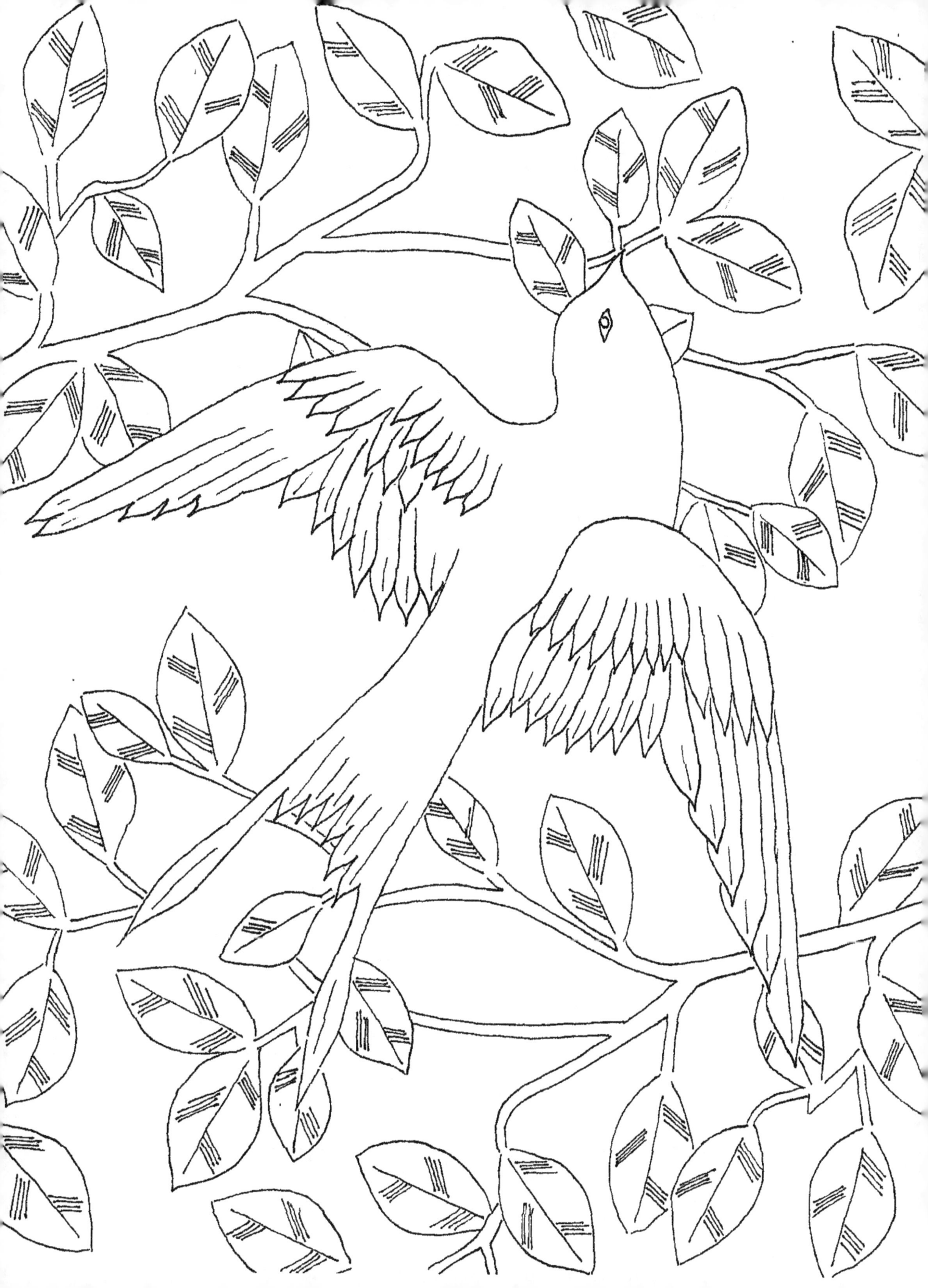

A journal is a good place to list possessions you are tired of owning.

Write in your journal feelings you are having right now.

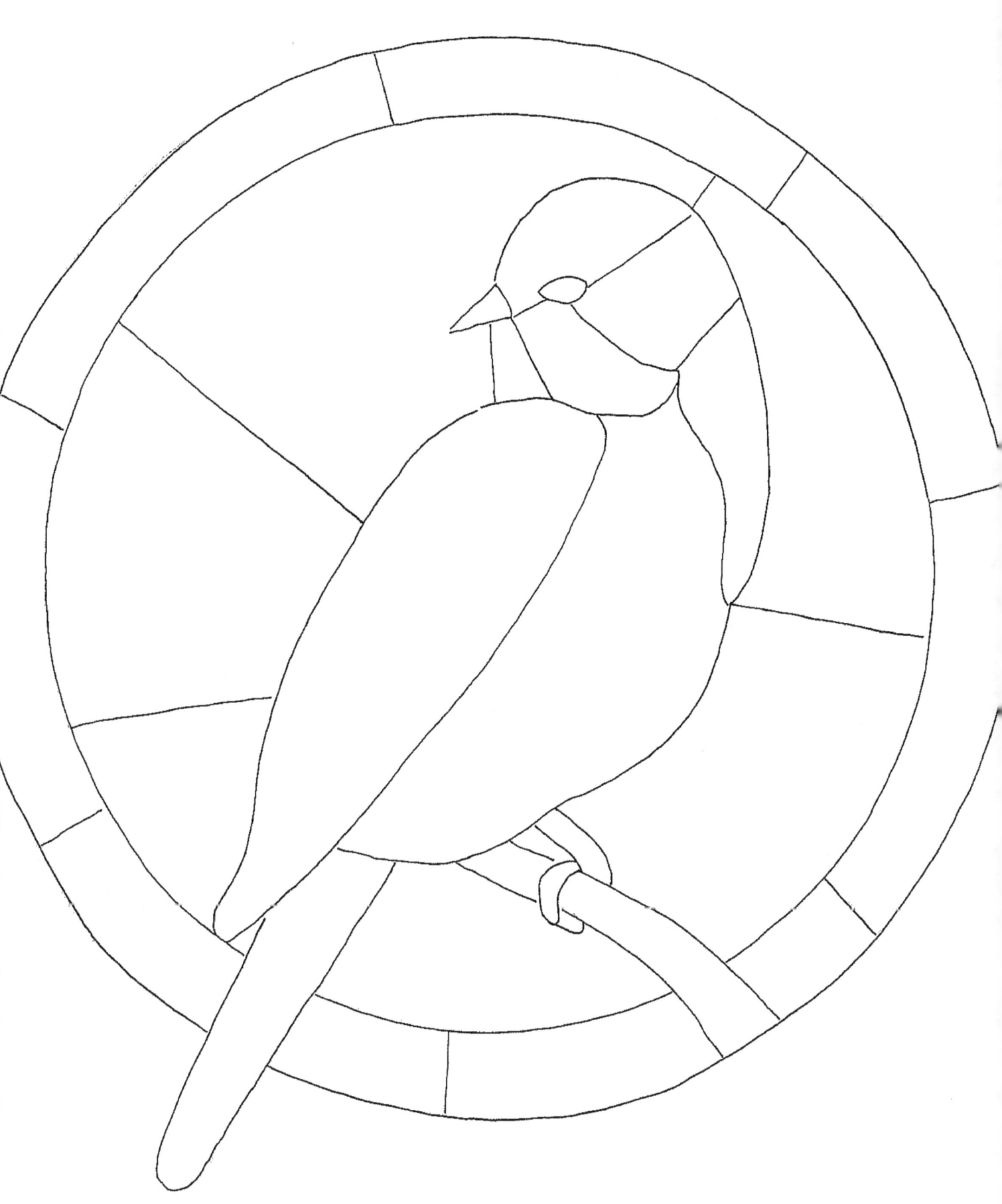

List things you would like for your child(ren) to know about you.

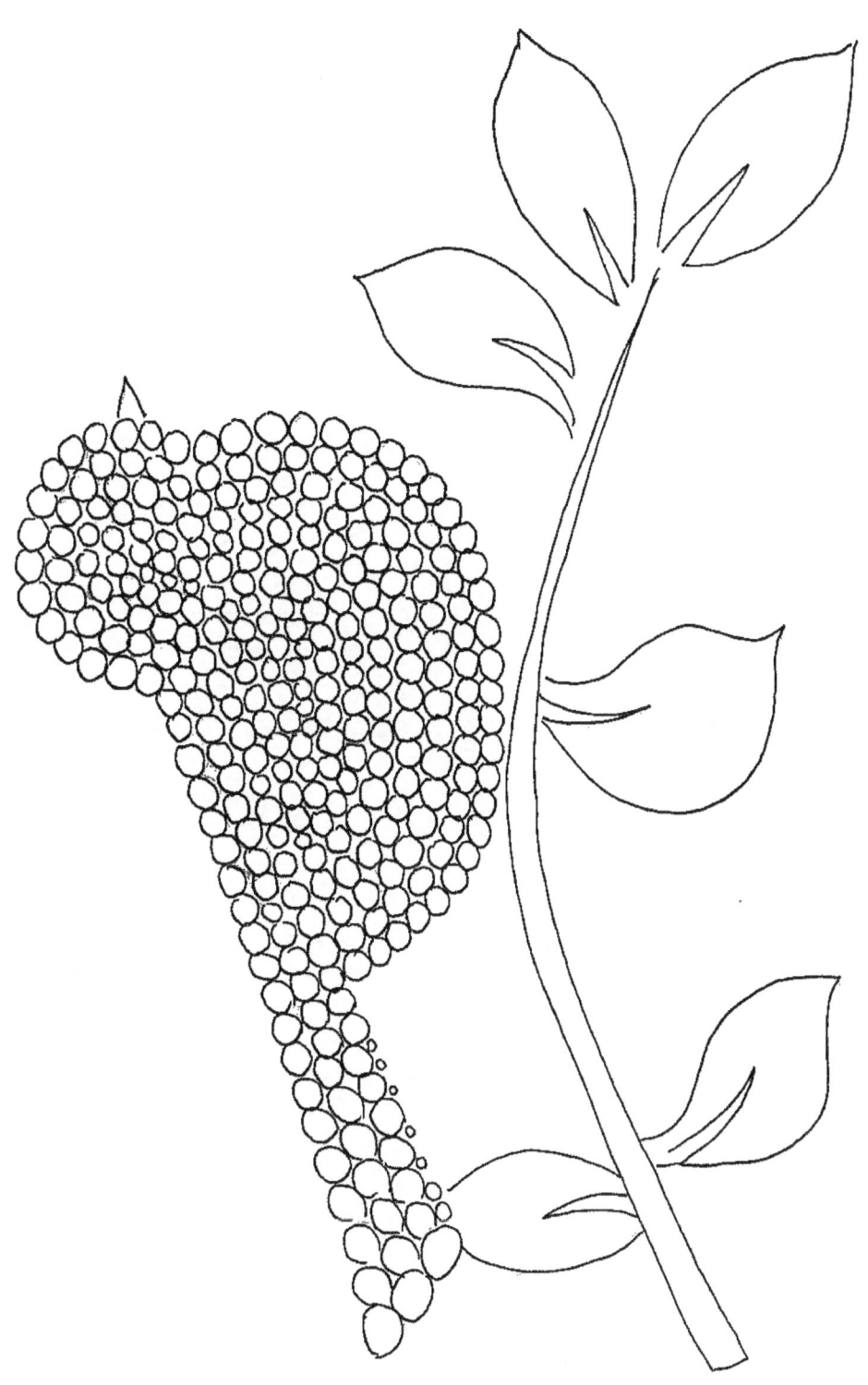

Make a list of things you are sad or angry about.

_____

_____

_____

_____

_____

_____

_____

_____

_____

_____

_____

_____

_____

_____

_____

_____

_____

_____

_____

_____

_____

_____

_____

_____

_____

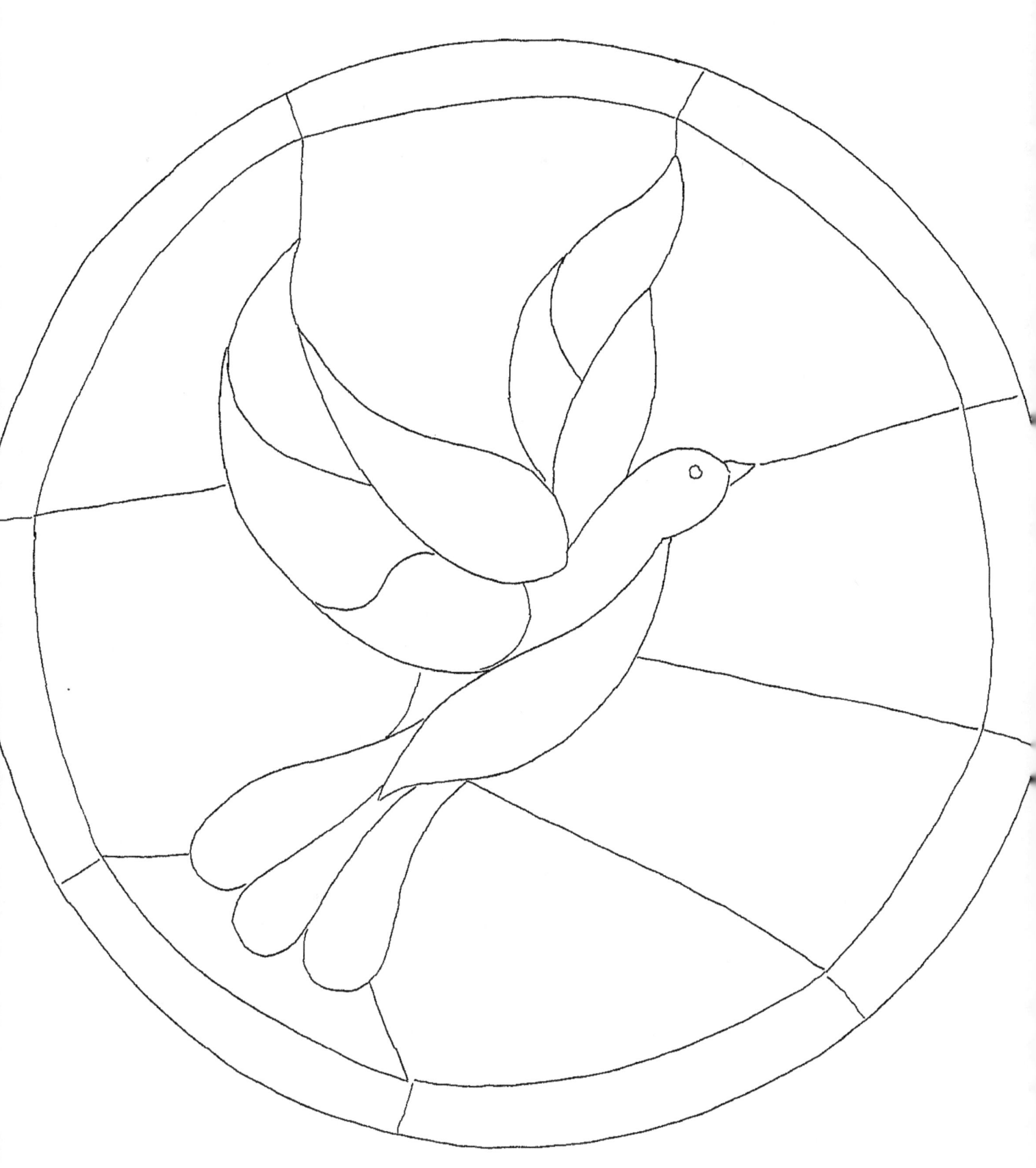

In your journal write things you would do if you were a millionaire.

www.ingramcontent.com/pod-product-compliance
Lightning Source LLC
Chambersburg PA
CBHW080613190526
45169CB00007B/2991